WILL THE REAL WOMEN
STAND UP!

PAT P.

BALBOA.PRESS

A DIVISION OF HAY HOUSE

Balboa Press books may be ordered through booksellers or by contacting:

Balboa Press
A Division of Hay House
1663 Liberty Drive
Bloomington, IN 47403
www.balboapress.com
1 (877) 407-4847

Because of the dynamic nature of the Internet, any web addresses or
links contained in this book may have changed since publication and
may no longer be valid. The views expressed in this work are solely those
of the author and do not necessarily reflect the views of the publisher,
and the publisher hereby disclaims any responsibility for them.

The author of this book does not dispense medical advice or prescribe the use
of any technique as a form of treatment for physical, emotional, or medical
problems without the advice of a physician, either directly or indirectly. The
intent of the author is only to offer information of a general nature to help
you in your quest for emotional and spiritual well-being. In the event you use
any of the information in this book for yourself, which is your constitutional
right, the author and the publisher assume no responsibility for your actions.

Any people depicted in stock imagery provided by Getty Images are
models, and such images are being used for illustrative purposes only.
Certain stock imagery © Getty Images.

Print information available on the last page.

ISBN: 978-1-9822-4927-4 (sc)
ISBN: 978-1-9822-4928-1 (e)

Balboa Press rev. date: 06/11/2020

Well, I would like to welcome you to my first book. There are more to come, so keep an eye out for them. I am a realist, so I write about things that are really happening today. And most of these issues many of us have to deal with everyday if not for ourselves, for a friend. So, to me, if you can't be real, then you must be fake, and I can't stand that!

Ok, ladies, you can see this book is dealing with you. Well, you are right. It's been a long time coming, ladies, and we really need a wake up call "NOW!" We are letting these men out here get away with too much. However, it seems as though men today have a code of ethics within themselves. But we ladies seem not to have this kind of code of behavior because we don't trust each other. Many women say that there is a shortage of decent men. So many of us are out on the prowl, and the attitude they have is: May the best one win.

Let's face it no one wants to be lonely. But is this really the right way? "Good Question?" "Right?" Don't worry. This question will be answered before this book is over. But before I go any further, I would like to give all honor and glory to "GOD ALMIGHTY." Most of all, I would like to thank, Him for his guidance and love. Now you are probably thinking, "Oh no! Here goes one of those Bible people again." Well, you are right, but there is balance for everything. In my opinion, the Bible even speaks of that. To me, people get it wrong. Just because you try to follow the Bible in your life does not mean you stop living your life. If that were the case, "God" would not have given it to us in the first place. But, He gave us his word as a guideline to help us in living our lives happily.

Many say to me, "Pat, how can you say that?" You know what I say to them? I tell them that God already knows what is inside my heart and mind, and you can't hide anything from Him, so let's just be real. He is not in a box. God created everything in this world, including us, so He knows what's best for us. And, as the Bible says, there is nothing new under the sun.

Now this book is going to touch on many issues, so get ready! Listen, fellas I love you, but some of you'll need to take stock and just stop with the madness. You will need to take an honest look at the way you view us as women and the way you treat us. Now I'm not saying all of you men are like this, but many of you are. We want our real men back! When a date was a date and not an expectation of something else from the lady simply because you took her out for an evening. We want the time back again when a man wanted to get to know a woman for who she is and to learn about the things she likes and doesn't like. To find out what hurts her or makes her happy, the simple things. When we first meet, let's go from A to B first instead of from A to Z. It is sad to say there's nothing left after the A to Z because both of you have shown your hand of cards. Game over, "NEXT!"

I believe this is the problem in our society today. We have forgotten how to fall in love. To feel that strong, throbbing feeling in your chest like you can't breathe and your heart is beating fast as soon as you see each other. Sometimes, these little things just build a strong and wonderful foundation in a relationship and maybe even lead to marriage. Because these are memories that you are building, like holding hands, your first kiss tells you, "Ok, that's it; slow it up. "HA! HA!" You are already at Z. See these are just those simple things which took you somewhere you didn't need to go. Maybe not for all of you, but it did happen for some of you. Don't lie; it did.

But see, these are some things we are missing, and it's breaking down our relationships and even our marriages. And if we, as grownups, are not doing these things and showing one anther respect and caring, how can we teach our children? Look at what our children see on television and hear on the radio. There are women being called out of their name?, including sexual implications and this is before some of them are even ready to date. This is not including the bad examples that many adults have already set for our young ones. We are the ones who should let them know when something is wrong because they are looking to us to do just that. They need our guidance. Many young people today are looking for our direction, especially if they have respect for you, so don't hold back. Give it to them. Teach your children about your values before someone else does who shouldn't.

Now some of you may be in an abusive relationship right now. But know this: God does not want this for you. God does not abuse you and neither should anyone else do so. So, this book should help you get out of this type of situation and many more dangerous and inappropriate situations in life. But know this: you will be encouraged and uplifted. The things we are going to discuss concern me, and are in my heart. And some of the things in this book you will find I, myself, have been through. And I'm not afraid to share my experiences with you.

Some say, "Girl, how do you put all your business out there like that?" My response to that is, "Somebody has to do it!" In all cases, God has helped me to get through it all. You know sometimes our eyes just need to be opened by God. Because He loves us and wants what is best for us. A lot of times we push things to go a certain way and then we say, "God has blessed me."

"WRONG!" Many times we have blessed ourselves with a big mess. This is especially true with relationships, ladies. We keep getting involved with the ones that are going nowhere. And the sad part about this is that we are aware of this and, yet, we still pursue it.

What is it? Are we that desperate for a man? That's a good question, isn't it? Well I'll let you answer that for yourself. And if we decide to go into a bad relationship anyway, then we get what we deserve because we came into it with open eyes. So, ladies, don't blame anybody else but yourselves. I've got to be hard on you because many of us just cry too much about how our man could have done this to us. "NO!" I say. How could you have done this to yourself? See, we can head off all of these problems before they even get started. First, we must know who we are in God. Once I found this out, then I knew what my purpose was in life. Talk about a great feeling, it's just fantastic. When God, starts to deal with you personally because you call on Him, to help you, just know this: He will. Let me ask you. Do you know who you are in God? Well let's save that question for later or maybe even another book.

What I am trying to get you to see is that, as a woman, you have rights. You have a right to be heard, respected and not treated like trash. Some of you have allowed this type of treatment to be done to you. Why, this was not God's, plan for you at all. And don't let anyone tell you differently. They are liars before God. Your life has purpose. As a matter of fact, everyone on this earth has a purpose of why they are here. The issue is sad, but many just don't care. Ok, ladies, let's start talking about some issues with these men today. Listen, if you have been dating someone for a year or two and have not yet met his parents or a relative: "RED LIGHT!" There's a problem. If he loved you, he would want to show you off to his family. To be honest, I feel that after six months, it should be enough time for him to know what he wants from you in a relationship. Now, ladies, I'm by no means saying to rush a man to marriage if he is not ready. For all you know, you may not be ready! And he may not be marriage material. I believe it is for these reasons that a lot of our marriages are not working out today. No one needs to be pushed into it if he or she is not ready. However, this does not give someone the right to just play with a person's feelings knowing there is no marriage in sight. As a matter of fact, some people don't even want to get married. These issues need to be discussed from the beginning.

Now, ladies, I have personally been through this with an ex-boyfriend. He knew I wanted to get married from the beginning, so he would toy with the idea. But the thing he didn't realize is that just because I wanted to get married didn't mean that he was the one. But, apparently, he thought he was. "SURPRISE!" Events didn't turn out that way and was I happy about that. In fact, it turned out he had a serious drug problem. You see, before I knew about his drug problem, he tried to play on my emotions. He wanted me to think he was interested in marriage too. Be careful with this because, in my opinion, he used this tactic to keep me hanging on to nothing. Yes, he wanted me, but he didn't want me for marriage nor did he want anybody else to have me either. This is selfish on a man's part to do this to woman, to keep her in a relationship which is going nowhere, so another man who may be ready to settle down, too, cannot pursue her because this guy who has no future plans to marry her is with her. So, she is hoping for something that she is never going to get. Sad, isn't it? But many of us fall for this type of foolishness all the time.

What about you ladies who have been with these types of men for 5,10, even 15 years and they have not married you yet? And you know what else makes me mad about this? Some of you have even given him kids. So, you are good enough to do the wifely things for him, but he is not man enough to marry you! "REALLY!" "REALLY!" Come on, ladies, we have got to change this. What are we doing? I'll tell you what we are doing; we are losing the respect that we deserve. What if our little girls are looking at this, and they will think it's normal? "WELL IT IS NOT!" Excuse me ladies, when you see these capital letters, I'm just mad. Then we wonder why these men of ours have 1,2,3, 4, children and sometimes more than that with other women. This kind of man can't run two households; he can't run the one he's at! Now, yes I know that things happen, but I hear some of you ladies say, "Oh he's at his other baby momma's house." Like you approve of this, and most likely he got this other girl pregnant while he was supposed to be committed to you. See you gave him all your cards A to Z, girlfriend, and now he has no respect for you. I know this is hard to hear, but let's not let our daughters go through this.

There is a woman that I know who was married to a man for over twenty something years. She gave him three children. She also said that they had been high school sweethearts. Well, he died and he left her with nothing despite the fact that he had a well-established job. They had a home together and children; it seemed picture perfect. As you can see, it was far from perfect. What we need to learn from this is that you must stand your ground on what you believe. Some of you may be wondering how long I was with my ex-boyfriend. Well, I was with him for almost two years. So, yes you can put up with this for a while, as I did. What a waste of time. I remember what an older lady told me once. She said to me, "Honey, wait on time because time will tell it all." You know what, she was right. What she was saying is that whatever he is not being honest about will come out later.

Again, now if the man you are seeing has not taken you to his house and you have been with him for quite some time, "RED LIGHT"! Guess what? It is a possibility that he is married or living with another woman whom you don't know about. Ladies, I hate to say this, but situations like this happen a lot these days. You think he's only into you and yet he has another life somewhere else with the other woman that you know nothing about. And you know what? Some of you accept this, and you are making it too easy for these guys to get away with this mess. If you can't have all of him, then you will not take half of him. Period. Reverse this situation on any man and see if he would put up with it. You know what he would say to you, "I'm not sharing you with anyone."

On the other hand, some men have many excuses for not introducing you to the family. This is what he may say if you question him about why he hasn't taken you to his house yet. He will most likely respond calmly and say let's plan to go next weekend. Then, of course, on that weekend something comes up. What about these men who want to see you only at night? So you mean to tell me that he couldn't come to visit you during the daytime? What about all those beautiful days that have passed by? But, yet, he says he loves and misses you. If that were really the case, he would want to spend quality time with you. I hate to say this, but to him, as seen by his actions, you are just a drive-by and you know what that means. What if he never takes you out in public? That could mean several things. He doesn't want to be seen with you, he's ashamed of you, or he has another woman.

Ladies, don't let these guys get away with this. Ask questions and watch how he treats you. You must demand your respect at all times. Remember ladies we never get too old to demand respect. Knowing this helps preserve us to age well. You don't abuse yourself, so neither should he. Disrespect is a form of abuse! The Bible says when you lay with a man, you give a portion of yourself to him. This is why it is hard to disconnect. This is what we call a broken heart. People don't like to admit it, but it is. Who would know better than our God? That is why he suggests marriage so people will be committed to each other. And most people marry for life. At least in the beginning that was the plan. Yes, things do change and some marriages don't work like they did in the earlier years. Statistics show that one out of every other marriage ends up in divorce. Something is not being applied somewhere.

Please know this: God is love and all He wants us to experience is his love in our everyday lives. God wants us to have this in our everyday activities. (1John 4-8) Many of you may say that you don't have a relationship like this with God, yet. Well, you can have one; the invitation is free. He just wants you to come to him in prayer. And then God will show you the way to go from there. You may say, "Why would God care about what is going on in my life? I'm not living right." Listen, many of us are not living perfect lives, but we are trying to get it right and none of us is perfect. We all have desires, some healthy some not. This is why we need God's guidance and love of forgiveness, so we can get it right. But where do we get direction about this?

From his word, the Bible. All God, wants us to do is to read it and research what we don't understand. And pray to Him for understanding as well, and it will be given to you through his holy spirit. You see, God has the power to make anything happen. Read the Bible. It says in Genesis that from God's voice alone He created the Earth and the things in it. Just his voice alone. Now that's a powerful God. He spoke it and it came to be. Once you know He is there with you, then you will start walking with Him, properly, and you will always want his approval at all times. Will we get it always? "NO"! I hate to bust your bubble but we are not perfect yet. This is why we go before Him, in prayer asking for his forgiveness. And He will be there for you every step of the way.

Next point, what if a guy tells you that he is in a relationship but it's not going too well? But he insists on wanting to continue seeing you? Don't fall for this. Never go into an already-made mess. Do not enter into a problem that you had nothing to do with in the first place. Meaning this current situation is not right at this time, so what can he offer you? "NOTHING!" But more mess. And you should not be second to anyone. Let him clean up his problems in the relationship he is in now. Then pray first for the answer, to fully understand if you should still continue being interested in this guy. Because you may want to "RUN!" It takes two to tango. Also a lot of guys like to have two or even more women and can't even handle the one they already have at home. All I'm saying is make sure you are free and so is he. Especially if he is married and if you touch that situation, you will block all your blessings. I can promise you that. How do I know? I was misled by a guy I used to date. I asked him from the beginning if was he married. He said no. This was just something I would automatically ask when I used to date. Because, even though it's hard to believe, many guys lie about being married. And some of them have lied so much about this that some of them actually seem as though they have even convinced themselves that they are not married. It's kind of funny when you think about it. But when it happened to me, I wasn't laughing. Of course, I believed him when he said he was not married, and then I fell in love with him. Then, guess what happened next? He said that he was married and that he thought he had told me. He knew he had never told me and so did I. So now I was in love with a liar, and I refused to let him go. Guess what my reasoning for staying in the relationship was? I stayed because he said that they were getting a divorce soon and that they were separated. So I felt this was ok. That was just foolish on my part. I now know that this man was not going to leave his wife for me. He had been playing this game forever. The men that date women while they are in a marriage just want their cake and ice cream too. Remember the wife always gets everything. And you know what? She should because she is married to the poor soul. It hurts me when I hear women say, "Oh, that's just the way men are. They are just feeling their oats, having a mid-life crisis." That's just foolishness ladies. If a woman conducted herself in a similar way, she would be considered a whore. But, in our culture, when referring to men cheating on their wives, some people say, OH IT'S JUST A MAN THING."

The scriptures say, Let no man pull apart what God, has put together. (Mark 10:5-9) If you both stand together on that, by not allowing yourself or anyone else or thing to come between you, then you will make it. Always fight for your marriage. Remember any arrangement that God created Satan wants it to fail. So that's another reason why marriages are so hard today. Every day is a fight to do what is right because there are temptations everywhere.

This brings me to another subject. There are many ladies out there who look for married men to be with. This is something I will never understand. Why would you purposely want to be number two? "SO WHAT?!" I say if he gives you money, pays your bills, and spends just weekends with you. Don't you want the whole package? Why do we sell ourselves short of all that God would bless us with? Not only that, this man is showing you what you are worth to him. For many men of this type, you are just a good time. But yet he tells you that you are something special to him. "LIES!" This is sad because you are confirming what he thinks of you by accepting his behavior towards you. He's never going to make you his wife, and if he ever did, he will do the same to you as he did to her. We forget what comes around goes around whether we like it or not. What also amazes me about these ladies who pursue married men is that the women may even know the wives. They will even brag about it to their friends. They maybe will smile in the wife's face as if she is her friend, knowing that she is sleeping with her husband. Don't just get mad at the woman. Also get mad at the man who is supposed to be faithful to his wife. Some men may look at this and believe that as long as they are still taking care of home, then everything is just fine. Well, a person may be taking care of home financially, but it takes more than that. You know there is an old song that I remember hearing a while ago and it goes something like this: "I was sneaking out the front door while she was sneaking out the back door!" It was written by a male songwriter, but I don't know his name. Now I don't believe in cheating at all in a marriage but it does happen. Remember what's good for one may be good for another. I'm just saying!

Next subject… The Bible says a man that does not work, let him not eat. Ladies, why are some of you taking care of these grown men? You get up to go to work, and he stays at your home. WHAT! Does your home need a babysitter? No! It needs someone to help contribute in paying its rent or mortgage. Another thing is that some of you have kids and these men take from the children. Believe me something is going to run short somewhere. Because you have someone costing you extra money, they are not helping you. First of all, in my opinion, this kind of man should not be living with you anyway. I hear so many women say, "I have been living with my boyfriend for x amount of years." I ask you, "Why?!" He doesn't know how good a woman you are yet? But I bet you cook for him, clean, even sleep with him, because you both are not in separate rooms. I don't mean to be hard on you ladies, but if you are doing these things, then you are his pretend wife. And what does this mean? It means you are doing everything a wife does except he is not married to you. You must set the stage from the beginning or your wishes will never be met. You will see others that you know getting married and you'll still be playing pretend wife.

Now back to the guy that wants to continue living off of you and tells you he can't get a job. This type of men just loves giving you a sad story. Don't fall for this. There are plenty of fast food restaurants, stores, construction jobs, etc. If he really wants a job, he can get one. The sad thing is he doesn't want to work. Why should he? You are doing everything for him. Also, I find this type likes to look for single women with children. Because he knows you are going to take care of your kids, no matter what. He knows those kids look to you to provide. And you know this. And, of course, a real mother would and does take care of her children. And, in most cases, the fathers are not helping or not around. Also, these guys figure you get lonely too. Come on, it's normal that you do because I did as well. We may be single but we are still human. And, of course, we are not dead, if you know what I mean. You still have needs and wants just like anyone else. But what you need to do with those needs and wants is a whole new story.

When I was going through this, I remembered what God said in the Bible. That He would not put more on me than I could bear. A lot of times we add extra pressure to our lives. We let this type of man in and we won't wait on God. The Bible says, Use discernment in your decisions no matter how good it looks. (Proverbs Ch.2:1-6) Because what we believe comes from God, may not have come from God. It's just our fleshly desires wanting to be met right then and there. Let's be real about this. We all have natural human feelings that arise at any time. Some of us wish sometimes that these desires would come but just not so often. Whatever you do, don't let your emotions or physical attractions cause you not to think. The biggest problem I have found is that, as women, we are more emotional than men are, so we react differently than they do. That is why you must stay alert and listen carefully to what He has to say.

The first date is really for getting to know each other, so you both are going to be on your best behavior. But give it time as you get to know one another, you will see the imperfections. And you will either talk about them or let them slide. And, ladies, for some, this is a problem because you may tell yourself that he is so fine! Also that he treats you so nicely, that he's crazy about you, and that he likes your kids, etc. And you know what the main one is? "It's hard to find a good man, so I'm not letting this one go." Now you are running on all emotions and the physical attraction. All I am saying is to keep your senses in order. You must see this guy for who he is and for who he is not. Most of all, ask him all the questions you can think of, even if they don't make sense. Listen to his response and look him in the eyes as he is speaking to you. If he can't look at you directly in the eyes while he is speaking to you, then most likely he is lying. If you don't understand his response, make him explain it to you. So there is no confusion. I believe this is why women get into abusive relationships. They don't ask important questions. Such as how do you feel about a man hitting on a woman? And in some relationships there is also the possibility of mental abuse which, to me, is worse than the physical abuse because sometimes you can't see it coming. The woman who subjects herself to this type of relationship usually has low self-esteem and she allows her partner to speak down to her all the time. He treats her as if her viewpoint is not important, and he has no respect for her at all. He shows this everyday in the way he treats her when they are alone and in front of others.

Then you have the other relationships where the men put on a show that everything is great, that there are no problems at all. While in reality, the woman hides the mental damage she deals with everyday. "HORRIBLE RIGHT?!" Yes, it is. And so many ladies are going through this on a regular basis. It could be someone at your job, a family member, friend etc. Ladies, whether it is physical or mental abuse, you must get out of this type of relationship. You can contact the center for prevention of abuse in your area. And they will help you from there.

Next point... I was talking to a client of mine. I'm a hairstylist, so you know in a salon we talk about many things. It is an open floor so to speak. Well, my client was saying that she went to a club where almost everyone there was married and creeping. Meaning out on a date, not with their husband or wife, and she admitted that she was one of them. I asked her how she could do this to her husband? She said, "Well, he started it, so I'm ending it." To me it sounded like a woman who has been hurt. But she did make it crystal clear to me that he is doing it too. So, I guess she is saying two wrongs make a right. After they both have done their dirt, they both come home and pretend no one has done anything wrong. I, personally, could not live like that. First of all, there are many diseases out there, and even more tragic, people are getting killed on the regular due to domestic disputes. And shame on the situation when one person is innocent and the other is not. Sad to say we have many situations like this. For some of this, ladies, we have ourselves to blame because we tolerate this type of behavior. Many of you say, "I know he is out in the streets, but as long as he comes home to me, I'll be alright." My question to you is, "ARE YOU CRAZY?!" "WILL YOU BE ALRIGHT?!" Yes, he may come home to you but he and what else will come back to you? For me, my life is way more important because if I'm dead, what can I do then? "NOTHING!"

It doesn't matter who is at fault because it usually starts out innocently. The man starts going out first with his buddies. And, of course, you don't mind at first. He may even ask, "Honey, me and the guys are going out tonight. Is that ok with you?" Of course, she tells him to go ahead and have a good time. But what happens is that it never stops. Almost every night he is out with the boys. Then she is left alone wondering what he is really doing. And every time he comes home from his evening out, then he wants to make passionate love to her to cover up what he has been doing. You see fellas, a woman knows when something isn't right, especially if you have been messing around. It is as if we can smell it. You know a "RAT!" Listen ladies and gents, both of you protect each other and what I mean by this is watch who you both hang with. Period. There are people out there who we call home wreckers, and they are out there just to do that. They will come off as your best friend, and most likely they are not happy in their own relationship at all. As a matter of fact, they are simply miserable and as you know, misery likes company. So they will try to break up your happy home. But they must gain your trust first, and once they do that, they will get to work on your household. They will accomplish this by causing confusion between you and your mate and maybe even flirting with your mate. At this point, they wll do anything that works. What it means is that they are jealous of what you have and if they can't have the same thing, then why should you? And this type of behavior can be done by a woman or a man. It doesn't matter. It happens all the time and usually by the one from whom you would least expect it.

How about this? You know this man hangs around your husband and knows your husband's schedule. So, what is he doing at your house knocking at your door while your husband is at work? And vice versa. Females can do the same thing. So, just remember a smile doesn't mean it is an innocent one at all. And your response to this knock should be, "Come back when my mate is here." Of course, speak these words through the door. (Don't even open the door. Period!) This could be a small thing to you, but this could become a large problem. You know people lie all the time. For instance, the uninvited visitor could say you let him in even though you may not have, etc. Just be careful who you and your mate associate with, and be sure to watch them for a while, their habits, actions and friends. Everything is not for everybody!

Ladies, can I ask you a question? Why are so many of you looking for a man? I hear all the time many of you saying, "Where are all the good men? I'm looking for one." Well, for one thing, you all are going about it the wrong way. Let God pick your man for you. The Bible says that a man that finds a wife is a good thing for him. It also says that a man will not abuse his own body; neither should he his wife. So God already has it planned out for you. You just need to be patient and wait. God even knows what you like in each area, and if you think he doesn't, you can tell him. But believe me he already knows. He knows your beginning and your end. You can even describe what type of man you want-sexually, physically, financially, mentally, etc. Be specific. It shows that you believe in Him to bless you regarding this matter. You notice the first point I mentioned is sexually. "WELL YES!" We want that area to be right and working! This is natural, ladies. Some of us have been waiting a long time. Not that we may not have control in that area, but let's just face the facts, we are not dead either. Wouldn't it be horrible on your wedding night if you find out, for whatever reasons, that your husband cannot perform sexually? Now that's a low blow, ha! A friend of mine married a guy and she thought he could perform sexually. Both claiming to be Christians, they decided to do what the Bible says and not have sex until marriage. Well, on the wedding night she said it was like peeling paint with her fingers, literally. They were never able to fix that area, so the marriage didn't last long. He was dishonest with her; he knew he could not perform. You see what I mean. Ask questions until you can get a clear answer.

And it is sad to say, my friend did ask and was still not told the truth. Many of us are lonely and just want a companion, and there is nothing wrong with that. But you must be careful and always take your time and, most of all, pray to God to ask what to do. Believe me, He will show you.

What about you ladies who are in physically abusive relationships? I have met at least three women in the last month who are running from their abusive mates. Some of them have even been threatened by these men. One of the ladies said that her mate threatened to kill her if he didn't hear from her in three months. While we were speaking, I was looking at her and I noticed there was a cut gash on her forearm almost a foot long. What kind of man would do this to a woman and say that he loves her? She said the last time he assaulted her, he tried to choke her to death. She said that she really thought her life was going to be over. She also has kids and she said she didn't want them to see this anymore. She could not bear to have her children watch her getting beaten for no reason, so she finally left this guy. It is a shame to me that many women like this one have to flee for their lives, along with her kids, to find safety and have some peace in their lives. To me, these guys need to be arrested and put in jail!

Furthermore, ladies, those of you who are going through this crisis, please keep paperwork on this guy. What do I mean? Fill out police reports, and if you do this, you will have documentation on the guy in case you may have to defend yourself and your children. Also, let him know that you will call the police on him. If he threatens you that you better not, wait until after the incident and file a report on him later. You see, ladies, this is your protection! I know of a situation of a lady friend of mine whose hair I used to do. She was in a horribly abusive relationship. Whenever she went out, after she came home, she had to be inspected by him (her husband) to check to see if her panties had a discharge from having sex. When she went out, she would also be given a strict time limit by him, and if she arrived home a minute late, she would face his jealousy and rage. Basically, he would beat her horribly. But the disturbing part about this is that she would tell me all of these things, but yet I saw no bruises. Then, she showed me that he would beat her in places that no one would be able to see: her stomach, back, upper arms, legs... You get the picture. Places where her clothing could hide the bruises. I would ask her why she would not call the police. She said he had threatened her that if she ever did, he would kill her dead. Period. He would also use her kids against her too. He would threaten her that he would harm her children, or take them away, etc. The thing about this lady was that she was simply just naturally gorgeous looking. But yet her esteem was so low she felt very unattractive, a sad fact which I just couldn't understand. But this man had been tearing her down for so long that she no longer had an identity of her own. "HOW SAD! HA!"

Pat P.

Well, one thing I helped her with is that she could still fill out a police report just to have on file for her own protection without him knowing. Because sometimes she had to literally fight this guy for her life at times. I counseled her to file a police report to have a clear record of her partner's physical abuse. This was to protect herself if, just say, things ever went bad for him, and for some reason, he was physically injured or even lost his life by her trying to protect herself or her kids. What would she do then? By filing a report beforehand, she would at least have proof in writing of the extensive abuse that she had been enduring, which could help support her in court.

Tragically, many women are in jail right now because they had no paper trail of what was going on with them in the abusive relationship. In addition, another sequence of events which is understandably irritating to the police is that you ladies call them for help, but when they ask you, "DO YOU WANT TO PRESS CHARGES?" YOU SAY, "NO!" In these cases, the police feel they have wasted their time. They could have answered another domestic violence call where charges would have been made. By missing another call, it is always possible that an abused woman might not make it because her abuser has killed her before the police could get there. Let's be clear, by no means am I suggesting that it is alright to take someone's life, but during domestic violence situations, lives have been lost. There are tragic examples of an abused woman trying to protect herself and she killed her abuser. Many women are in jail because they had no written proof of their partners' physical assaults and abuse, such as prior police reports. And that is a very, very, sad situation doing time for something that really wasn't entirely her fault because she was forced to defend herself. Well, ladies, this is another issue.

First of all, can I ask some of you out there a question? Do you have children? For those of you who say yes, I would like for you all to just think about what I'm saying. I also have two daughters, and I raised them practically by myself. Was it hard? "YES IT WAS HARD!" But I never gave up because I knew God was with me the whole time. I knew my children were my responsibility. The first one I had was planned, and I never thought the dad and I would later get a divorce, but we did. Of course, life still goes on and that child still needs to be taken care of. But some of you feel someone owes you something with helping you to take care of your kids. I heard a girl literally curse her mother out because she could not take care of her four children for the night so she could go out with her girlfriends. Her mother already looked extremely tired and sickly. Do you think this girl cared? "NO!" Instead, she had an attitude and left the children anyway and didn't leave any clean clothes or food. Now, I am going to get real with you ladies who create this kind of mess right here. First of all, your mother did not lay down and have those kids; you did. You knew what you were doing when you were doing it. Also, ladies, what is wrong with protection not just from getting pregnant but also from getting some sexual transmitted diseases? Pleasure is not worth your life. Also, it is not worth bringing a life into the world knowing you cannot care for a child. Yes, it is great to have mom there to help out, but remember she has already raised you and if you have siblings, she has raised them too. Don't you think she is tired now? What about her aging well? She already has the stress of taking care of herself, and now you are asking her to worry about your stress too. That is just too much!

When I had my kids, I would bring them over for my mom to enjoy their company not to babysit them, and I was there the whole time. Now, did I need my mom to ever babysit for me? I asked her very rarely and only if it was an emergency. Now I know there are some mothers out there who want to babysit their grandkids and be a part of their lives, and I think that is great. But you new moms should not think you are owed anything because you are not. You made your bed; now you have to lie in it. Some of us make mistakes in life, but it does not mean you cannot overcome them because you can. Many of us have overcome our mistakes and moved forward in our lives. And if your mother is helping you out with your children, give her a hug and say thank you. Thank you are two words that can go a long way ladies. I have a friend who asked me why it is so hard to leave a man that you really love. Especially if you know that he is no good for you. I responded to her that it is like an addiction and you feel you just can't do without him. And if you have been with this guy for a long time, it makes it even harder to let go. And if he knows this, he will play a game with you just to keep you around for whatever reason. If he knows this, he will use it to benefit him. Also, many women don't want to be alone. And please don't let her be getting older in age or, as many say, her clock is ticking and there is no turning back. Then what happens? She panics and she starts thinking about children, marriage, the future, etc. It is understandable, especially if you keep getting invited to your friends' weddings as one of the bridesmaids, and as you walk down the aisle, you are wishing it was your wedding. You tell yourself every time, I am not going to do this to myself again. But the next wedding comes, and you say yes again to participate, and then afterward you go home depressed. You bring the wedding up to your man, on the sly, just to get his response. And he responds to you with one-word answers, letting you know that he really doesn't want to talk about this right now. Period. You go to sleep crying again from his reaction. But you know deep down inside he is not the one for you. But you have been with him for several years now.

So what should you do? Well, this is my opinion, but since you have been with this man for a long period of time, then maybe it is time for a thorough evaluation of this fellow. You need to determine if he is really marriage material at this point in the relationship. And, at this moment, you can't say you don't know enough about him since you have been with him for a long time now. Time tells a lot about a person because things always come out as people get to know each other. Like I said earlier, no one should be rushed into marriage. But at the same time it's not fair to be in a married setting and yet there is no marriage in sight. You are playing the role well, but where is your paperwork? So, sometimes this can be a reason for not wanting to leave a relationship because it feels normal to be with this man. You are together all of the time; you may even have children with him. So you are in a family setting and you want what is best for your children.

I was in a relationship with a man who just loved our kids and would show them so much love. He even planned outings for them, pizza days, etc. But yet for me he would treat me horribly. We would start out good at first with so much love in the air. But give it a good week and here we were again arguing and fighting, etc. And when the fighting was over, I realized that it was usually over something small, nothing important. I had to evaluate this because even though he was great with our kids, he treated me horribly, sometimes in front of them. And I just refused to put up with that. Period. I realized that in my relationships, the guy is going to respect me at all times, the same way he wants me to do for him. I had to admit to myself that we were like water and oil; we just couldn't mix.

Nobody has a right to mistreat anybody especially in front of the children! Now I know everyone has their way of doing things in a relationship, but as for me, respect me or the highway. Because once you lose that, you have nothing. And if they see the father disrespecting you, most likely the children are going to do it too. Just give it time. I say this because children practice what they see and hear. One day I was in the store and there was a little boy there about five years old. He was literally cursing his mother out because he couldn't get what he wanted. To be that young and to use such abusive language, he had to have heard someone in his family talking to his mother that way. And the name he was calling her was horrible. All I can say is, "He couldn't have been mine talking to me that way!" Now this is my opinion as well as it is written in the Bible: Do not spare the rod. That means don't hold back from discipline for any child who deserves it. The Bible also says that a child who is not disciplined will cause his mother great pain and will make her cry. Then when the child grows up and becomes a problem in society the first thing that is said, Where were his parents? And, what kind of upbringing did he have? The Bible says that you bring up a child from infancy according to the word, the Bible, so as to show him or her which way to go. This is the parent or parents' responsibility. So, again, it does matter who you decide to marry because he may not want to raise his children this way.

Another reason why many women can't or won't leave a man is because he is very controlling. And this behavior can be controlling mentally or physically; neither behavior is good. This is a situation where whatever he says goes, whether she likes it or not. Her opinion doesn't matter to him. And when she speaks, she needs to be careful of what she says. This is his way of breaking her down, so she will never go against him. This is a bad relationship to be in. First, this kind of partner breaks the mind down, then the physical may come in if the woman ever tries to buck him on anything that he does not like. It doesn't matter if she has a problem with what he is upset with her about. The point is that he will not tolerate her questioning him, and she is expected to have no opinion at all. Like don't speak unless you are spoken to type of relationship. And God bless her if she makes a decision without his permission; there will be a problem. This is a very abusive relationship and, sad to say, this goes on everyday. This woman may want to leave but she doesn't know how. My opinion is that she should call a battered women's shelter, and they should know what to do and how to help her. If you have children, please let them know that. Remember when you embark on this you must be serious. You have many peoples' lives involved in this. "DON'T PLAY!" Make sure when you make the decision to move, you move and do not hesitate! The people who work in shelters put their lives on the line to help you, remember that. They don't know you and they don't know him.

Another reason to be sure to make your move and not hesitate is that he can be very persuasive and manipulative to convince you to stay. He may try to manipulate you by bringing up old times, the things you both used to do. Also, he may try to use other manipulative tactics, such as telling you that you can't live without him or that you have all been together too long to separate now! Basically, it's all a big guilt trip, so you will second-guess yourself, so you decide to stay with him and there you will be for another year in an abusive relationship! Nothing will have changed; everything will still be the same. Then you wonder why you can't move forward because you will not step out on faith.

Remember time is wasting! There comes a time when you have to take control of your life. This may seem hard at first, but sometimes you need to get out of a situation, so you can see it clearly from the outside. Also time is a good healer, so your mind can become stronger, and you will be able to tell if something is not good for you. The mind is tricky if you have been dealing with someone who knows how to manipulate it. He know what makes you tick. You are his puppet until you say, "NO, NOT ANYMORE! THAT IS ENOUGH!!!!!!!"

At this point, I just want to encourage you all right now. Listen, many of us have stories to tell about our lives, including me. But, if we do not learn from the stories of others and from our own stories and we do not progress to do better, then we have not grown and we cannot press forward in health and well-being. Please know this: You can do it. One thing that is true is if the people around you are not encouraging you, then get away from them. Remember, misery loves company. Some other people are not happy and they don't want you to be happy either. Also, ladies, if you can't find the answer to any of the things we have discussed in this book or feel you don't have the strength to make a decision about these things right now, just PRAY!!!!!!!!!!!!! God, created you, so he knows everything about you, and he will know when you will be strong enough to make your move. You see there is nothing new under the sun to him. He knows everything! You know what He likes to say to me through his holy spirit when I have a serious problem? I love this quote. He says, "Patricia I don't move half mountains. I move whole mountains!" Powerful, isn't it? His words mean that he will handle the whole problem, not just part of it.

Now some of us are in toxic relationships and that could be with anyone-a woman or a man. So this can apply to a family member, co-worker, girlfriend, guy friend, etc. What do you think of when you hear the word toxic? I think of poison, something that is not good for me. It can harm me. Yes, these are some strong words, but they can apply to some people that you deal with on a daily basis. You know a certain person is not good for you, but you deal with him or her anyway. You may go to dinner with the person, a movie, etc. And you know before you go you shouldn't because that person is going to do something to really make you mad or make a comment to upset you. It never fails even when you try to give someone the benefit of the doubt. And these types of people are like magnets. They just will not let go. They feel that you are their best friend and they are the same to you. But yet they treat you like a dirty, old dishtowel. For example, they will pay you a compliment but then turn around and say something negative right after it. Or, they may bring up something very hurtful to you that you had discussed with them and you thought it would never be mentioned again. This kind of person loves to catch you off guard. This person is very jealous of you, and he or she looks forward to hurting you. This type of toxic relationship is also a controlling one. From the beginning, you really believe that this person is a real friend because they seem to be so nice. But as time passes, it is as if the person is taking jabs at you until he or she sets you up for the knockout punch. It comes from out of nowhere; you didn't see it. I find that people like this either had someone do this to them or they just acquired the technique and know how to use it on whoever they please.

This kind of toxic relationship can also happen between a child and a parent, and it can be very difficult for the child. Because a child wants the parents' approval and it is very important to a child at an early age. But some parent-child relationships just don't work. For example, the parent may favor the youngest over the oldest, something that is not right, but it happens. So the oldest will try everything to please his or her parent but nothing changes. So the oldest child has resentment in his or her heart and this situation becomes toxic. In such cases, the parent either does something to fix this problem and love each child for who they are, because each child is different, or there will be problems, and the negative effects can follow that child into adulthood. That is why in many families we have sibling rivalry, which is not good. The children are always trying to prove to each other that one is better than the other. And please don't let the adults be an audience that really gets and keeps this toxic family dynamic going. In this case, let's hope the parents can encourage the children to love each other because if they hate one another, this really creates a toxic relationship. I am not saying that it cannot be corrected, but it is going to take some time and effort on both the parents' and the siblings' part.

However, since this book has been mostly written for women I would like to talk about us in toxic so-called friendships with each other. Some of us are so desperate for female friends that we will go through anything to have them whether it is healthy or not. One thing that we must remember is that each person is different in her personality. You need to find out if you both have the same interests. A lot of times you may find you both have nothing in common at all! She may be a gossiper but you are not; that could create a problem. Because if she is talking about others to you that you both know, then most likely she is talking about you too. There is already a trust issue there. What about the type that just gets on your nerves the whole time she is around you? She just makes you want to cringe and go home. You two have never hit it off! But, sad to say, even with these types of incompatible personalities I have just mentioned, we still decide to put up with the problems and we continue to hang with them. And then when someone does something to offend you, then you run to everyone to talk about what she did. Ladies, these are toxic relationships. Some people need to stay as associates only. Meaning if they are at your job, leave them there on the job. Now, I am not saying you can't make great friends at work because you can and I have. But some things need to stay at work when you leave work. Also women have a tendency just to be messy. And I don't know why that is but it's true. I am a hairstylist and in a beauty shop, you see it all and hear it all. I feel that I have a bit of authority to say what I just said because of that. Ladies, we used to have a sisterhood. What happened to that? We stuck together because we are women, and we had each other's backs. And we get so jealous of one another so quickly over little things that it is just pitiful. What ever happened to being happy for the other person and wishing her well? Sad to say, we don't see much positiveness anymore as the world is changing and so are the people within it. Yes, there are many doing good things, but there are also many people who are not. The Bible says in the last days there will be critical times hard to deal with. (2Tim.3:1-4) And we see this every day when we turn on the news, etc. The Bible says many will have no natural love for each other. It's more like you get yours and I will get mine. Also some people have wrong motives when they do things for others, and a lot of times it is for personal gain.

Some of you may be asking, so what about men in toxic friendships with other men? Well, I believe men can disconnect more easily than women can. Why do I say that? It is because, as I said earlier, men are more logical than emotional. So, if they are in a friendship that is causing problems or is not good for them, they will often walk away from it and will say, "I am done with that." And, sad to say, they will do it faster than women will. Now, if he is really in love with a woman and they break up for whatever reasons, then he may become more emotional. And this is because his heart and feelings are involved. Some men have even cried over a woman, especially if she was good to him. Therefore, even though they are often more logical than we are, they still have feelings. Remember this is just my opinion. You don't have to agree with me. But in most cases people do.

Now ladies, back to you. What if your man just doesn't want you anymore?! How do you disconnect? Now that, for many, can be very difficult. The first thing, don't be stalking the man. Don't laugh. You all know that you be doing this. I have even done it. I knew he was with another woman, so I sat out in the parking lot until he came out. How about driving around to different hotels to see if his car is there? Ok, you find him there, so what is next? You look like an idiot! And you know what is the shame about all of this? If he is with another woman, we want to fight her. Why?! You were with him and he made the decision to be with her. The questioning and anger should be with him, not her. I had one woman tell me that if she caught her man out with another woman, she would beat her behind. She did not say these exact words but you get my point. I asked her why? It is not the woman's fault. She said that she did not care and that she would beat her so badly until she would never want to go out with her man again. I looked at her like she was a fool! I then asked her how she would feel and what she would do if the other woman did not know that she was with another woman's man. This fool said, "Well, she will know now, so she won't mess with him anymore."

I just feel a lady should always be a lady in any situation. Handle it in a dignified and classy way. Never, ever let a man see you sweat, knowing he has done you wrong. You are the innocent one, not him. And to you ladies that are married and this type of mess is going on, you don't let him see you sweat either! And when I say this, what I mean is don't let him break you. You show him that you are a strong woman and until you decide to change your last name back to your maiden name, you will demand respect from him. Because you are still his wife! And if you have children with him, you are still the mother of his kids. Don't let him see you cry; go to a close friend or family member for that. Right now you have to make him wonder. "What's On Her Mind Right Now?!" Girl, keep him in suspense until you are ready to talk to him. He has no rights at this point and don't be so quick to lay with him either because you are not sharing your husband with anyone. You need to have a talk with him to find out where his head is first. Don't go off; stay cool and calm to whatever he says. But remember, you have to see if this is something that you can forgive and live with. In many cases, it is too much, but for some, it can be worked out. That will be your decision. Don't go asking your girlfriends, your momma, your daddy, etc. They are there to be your listening ears only. Let's face it, they don't have to live with the situation; you do.

Now, during this time your husband is going to want to know what you are thinking. He will want to know if you are you going to walk or stay. He is going to want to talk to you, either to end it or work it out. Because, remember, I told you to stay cool and calm and not to say much. In my opinion, this is therapy because it helps him to look at what he did to you, and if you have children, what he did to his whole family. Basically, at this point, he does not know where he stands with you right now. So this is making him a bit nervous about his family situation and where it is heading. I feel if he is going to put you through all of these changes, then he needs to go through some too! Ladies, we make it too easy for these guys to get back in after they have done wrong. If his infidelity is not serious to you, then it is not serious to him. If all you are worrying about is keeping your marriage together, you are going to have some long, long, nights. You are probably asking why? Because if you haven't gotten down to why he did what he did, you are still at square one. That is why it is so important during this process to not say much and to let him do all the talking. I promise you he is going to spill the beans. A man cannot handle pressure like this, and he will lose it. And that's what you want him to do, so he can tell it all. Also, this will let you know where he stands with you. Because he has had time to think about all of this and either he is going to stay or walk. You be prepared for either way because you have your standards, as well, about what you are going to put up with and not.

You see, ladies, we get drowned, so to speak, in our families' lives and forget that we have a life too. When you marry, you are investing your life in that relationship. And if there are children, that is more of your life that you invest. I hate to sound like you are putting money in a bank, but in a way you are. You are just hoping that it doesn't go bankrupt! Sad to say, many have. But that is just life. Many people have gone through it and are going through it right now. You will be no different than the next person. But if you can work it out, by all means do. Please do one thing for me. Listen closely and make him explain everything. And you look right into his face so you can see his eyes as he is speaking to you. You want eye contact, and if he cannot look you in yours as he is speaking to you, then there is a great possibility he is lying to you. Then, I would go back into cool and calm mode, meaning not saying much, and if this continues on for a long time, then maybe you should walk. Remember, he is the one who broke the marriage vow, ...*until death do us part!* Nobody is dead yet! And if he can't be faithful to you, then he needs to walk and not continue to waste your life any longer. Life is precious people; it can be here today and gone tomorrow. "So Why Waste IT?!"! Live IT! Love IT! and Like IT! Anyone who has a problem with this, go jump in a lake and cool off. You will be alright.

Now, gentlemen, this advice is not just for women. You can apply it, too, if you are in a similar situation. We may do another book for you later. Right now I am concerned about the ladies. Finally, ladies, I want to encourage you. I have some final questions for you. "WHO ARE YOU?" "WHAT DO YOU WANT OUT OF LIFE?" Once you can honestly answer these questions, I believe that you can move forward and heal. And if no one wants to get in the wagon with you, "KICK THEM OUT!" My sisters, whether black or white, we are all women who have a story to tell. I love you all and may, God bless every move that you make small or large. "YOU JUST GO GIRL!"

Printed in the United States
By Bookmasters